CW01582718

This series prepared in
consultation with the
British Veterinary Association
Animal Welfare Foundation

© Rod Campbell 1990
First published 1990 by
Campbell Books
96 Leonard St · London EC2A 4RH
in association with The Watts Group
All rights reserved
ISBN 1 85292 053 X
Printed in Singapore
10 9 8 7 6 5 4 3 2 1

We have a Cat

Rod Campbell

CAMPBELL BOOKS

We have a cat.
I love it very much and
like helping to look
after it . . .

Cats need two meals
a day, but kittens need
feeding more often.
I help to feed my cat
fish, meat, and milk in
its own bowl.

My cat doesn't make a mess
on the floor.
It uses a special tray
or goes outside through
the cat-flap.

I pick up my cat very carefully and put it down very gently.

My cat likes to play.
It likes things that
move and make a noise.

My cat doesn't need
a bath because it cleans
and washes itself.

To keep my cat well, we always visit the Vet. The Vet is the animals' doctor.

My cat needs a nice
warm bed.
It sleeps in the kitchen.

Shh...I think it's asleep now!
Can you see?